EMMANUEL JOSEPH

The Social Contract of Health, Political, Psychological, and Business Perspectives on Wellness

Copyright © 2025 by Emmanuel Joseph

All rights reserved. No part of this publication may be reproduced, stored or transmitted in any form or by any means, electronic, mechanical, photocopying, recording, scanning, or otherwise without written permission from the publisher. It is illegal to copy this book, post it to a website, or distribute it by any other means without permission.

First edition

This book was professionally typeset on Reedsy. Find out more at reedsy.com

Contents

1. Chapter 1: Introduction to the Social Contract of Health — 1
2. Chapter 2: Historical Foundations of the Social Contract... — 3
3. Chapter 3: Political Perspectives on Health — 4
4. Chapter 4: Psychological Perspectives on Health — 5
5. Chapter 5: The Role of Businesses in Promoting Health — 6
6. Chapter 6: Health Equity and Social Justice — 7
7. Chapter 7: Public Health and the Social Contract — 8
8. Chapter 8: Mental Health and Well-Being — 9
9. Chapter 9: The Economic Impact of Health — 10
10. Chapter 10: Health Communication and Education — 12
11. Chapter 11: The Role of Technology in Health — 13
12. Chapter 12: Health Systems and Infrastructure — 14
13. Chapter 13: Global Health and the Social Contract — 15
14. Chapter 14: Ethical Considerations in Health — 16
15. Chapter 15: Health Policy and Advocacy — 17
16. Chapter 16: The Future of the Social Contract of Health — 18
17. Chapter 17: Conclusion and Call to Action — 20
18. Chapter 18: The Role of Cultural and Social Factors in... — 21

1

Chapter 1: Introduction to the Social Contract of Health

The concept of health is multidimensional, encompassing physical, mental, and social well-being. It is not merely the absence of disease or infirmity but a state of complete wellness. In society, health is a collective responsibility that involves individuals, communities, and institutions. This chapter explores the notion of health as a social contract, examining how political, psychological, and business perspectives intersect to promote wellness.

The idea of a social contract in health implies a mutual agreement among members of society to uphold and support each other's well-being. This contract is not formalized in legal terms but is rooted in social norms and ethical principles. Governments, healthcare providers, businesses, and individuals each play a role in fulfilling this contract. The chapter will delve into the historical and philosophical foundations of the social contract theory and its application to health.

From a political perspective, the social contract of health involves the government's responsibility to ensure access to healthcare services, create policies that promote public health, and protect citizens from health threats. This includes addressing social determinants of health such as education, employment, and environmental factors. The chapter will discuss various political ideologies and their approaches to health, highlighting the role of public policy in shaping health outcomes.

Psychological perspectives on health emphasize the importance of mental well-being and the impact of social and environmental factors on psychological health. This chapter will explore theories of stress, coping mechanisms, and the role of social support in maintaining mental health. It will also discuss the importance of mental health awareness and the need for integrating psychological well-being into the broader concept of health.

2

Chapter 2: Historical Foundations of the Social Contract Theory

The origins of the social contract theory can be traced back to the works of philosophers such as Thomas Hobbes, John Locke, and Jean-Jacques Rousseau. These thinkers proposed that individuals come together to form societies based on mutual agreements, with the goal of ensuring collective well-being and protection. This chapter will provide an overview of the key principles of social contract theory and its evolution over time.

In the context of health, the social contract theory has been applied to understand the responsibilities of individuals and institutions in promoting public health. The chapter will explore how historical events, such as the rise of public health movements and the establishment of healthcare systems, have shaped the modern understanding of health as a social contract.

Finally, the chapter will discuss contemporary interpretations of social contract theory in the context of health. This includes examining the role of global health organizations, international agreements, and the impact of globalization on health outcomes. The chapter will provide a comprehensive understanding of how the social contract theory continues to shape health policies and practices.

3

Chapter 3: Political Perspectives on Health

The political landscape plays a crucial role in shaping health policies and determining access to healthcare services. This chapter will explore different political ideologies and their approaches to health, including the role of government intervention, the balance between public and private healthcare systems, and the impact of political decisions on health outcomes.

The chapter will discuss the role of public policy in addressing social determinants of health, such as education, employment, and housing. By examining case studies from various countries, the chapter will highlight the successes and challenges of different policy approaches in promoting public health.

The chapter will also explore the relationship between politics and health equity. By analyzing the distribution of resources and access to healthcare services, the chapter will discuss the ethical implications of health disparities and the need for policies that promote health equity.

Finally, the chapter will discuss the role of political advocacy and activism in shaping health policies. This includes examining the impact of grassroots movements, non-governmental organizations, and international health organizations in promoting health and well-being.

4

Chapter 4: Psychological Perspectives on Health

Mental health is a critical component of overall well-being, and psychological perspectives provide valuable insights into the factors that influence mental health. This chapter will explore theories of stress, coping mechanisms, and the role of social support in maintaining mental health.

The chapter will discuss the impact of social and environmental factors on psychological well-being, including the effects of poverty, discrimination, and social isolation. By examining these factors, the chapter will highlight the importance of addressing social determinants of mental health.

The chapter will also explore the role of mental health awareness and education in promoting psychological well-being. This includes discussing the importance of reducing stigma, increasing access to mental health services, and integrating mental health into broader health initiatives.

Finally, the chapter will discuss the need for a holistic approach to health that integrates physical, mental, and social well-being. By emphasizing the interconnectedness of these dimensions, the chapter will highlight the importance of a comprehensive approach to health and wellness.

5

Chapter 5: The Role of Businesses in Promoting Health

Businesses play a significant role in promoting health and well-being, both through their internal policies and their impact on the broader community. This chapter will explore the responsibilities of businesses in promoting health, including workplace wellness programs, corporate social responsibility, and the ethical implications of business practices on health.

The chapter will discuss the role of businesses in addressing social determinants of health, such as employment, income, and working conditions. By examining case studies of businesses that have successfully promoted health, the chapter will highlight best practices and lessons learned.

The chapter will also explore the relationship between business practices and health outcomes. This includes examining the impact of marketing, product design, and supply chain practices on public health. By analyzing these factors, the chapter will discuss the need for businesses to adopt health-promoting practices.

Finally, the chapter will discuss the role of partnerships between businesses, governments, and non-governmental organizations in promoting health. By highlighting successful collaborations, the chapter will emphasize the importance of a multi-sectoral approach to health and wellness.

6

Chapter 6: Health Equity and Social Justice

Health equity is a fundamental aspect of the social contract of health, and this chapter will explore the ethical implications of health disparities. By examining the distribution of resources and access to healthcare services, the chapter will discuss the need for policies that promote health equity.

The chapter will discuss the role of social justice in promoting health, including the importance of addressing social determinants of health and reducing health disparities. By examining case studies of successful initiatives, the chapter will highlight best practices and lessons learned.

The chapter will also explore the role of advocacy and activism in promoting health equity. This includes examining the impact of grassroots movements, non-governmental organizations, and international health organizations in advocating for health equity and social justice.

Finally, the chapter will discuss the need for a comprehensive approach to health that integrates social, economic, and environmental factors. By emphasizing the interconnectedness of these dimensions, the chapter will highlight the importance of a holistic approach to health and wellness.

7

Chapter 7: Public Health and the Social Contract

Public health is a critical component of the social contract of health, and this chapter will explore the role of public health initiatives in promoting wellness. By examining the history of public health movements, the chapter will highlight the successes and challenges of different approaches to public health.

The chapter will discuss the role of public health policies in addressing social determinants of health, such as education, employment, and housing. By examining case studies from various countries, the chapter will highlight best practices and lessons learned.

The chapter will also explore the impact of public health emergencies, such as pandemics and natural disasters, on health outcomes. By analyzing the response to these emergencies, the chapter will discuss the importance of preparedness and resilience in promoting public health.

Finally, the chapter will discuss the role of global health organizations and international agreements in promoting public health. By highlighting successful collaborations, the chapter will emphasize the importance of a multi-sectoral approach to public health.

8

Chapter 8: Mental Health and Well-Being

Mental health is a critical component of overall well-being, and this chapter will explore the factors that influence mental health. By examining theories of stress, coping mechanisms, and the role of social support, the chapter will provide valuable insights into the importance of mental health.

The chapter will discuss the impact of social and environmental factors on psychological well-being, including the effects of poverty, discrimination, and social isolation. By examining these factors, the chapter will highlight the importance of addressing social determinants of mental health.

The chapter will also explore the role of mental health awareness and education in promoting psychological well-being. This includes discussing the importance of reducing stigma, increasing access to mental health services, and integrating mental health into broader health initiatives.

Finally, the chapter will discuss the need for a holistic approach to health that integrates physical, mental, and social well-being. By emphasizing the interconnectedness of these dimensions, the chapter will highlight the importance of a comprehensive approach to health and wellness.

9

Chapter 9: The Economic Impact of Health

The economic impact of health is a critical aspect of the social contract of health, and this chapter will explore the relationship between health and economic outcomes. By examining the cost of healthcare services, the chapter will discuss the importance of addressing economic factors in promoting health.

The chapter will discuss the role of businesses in promoting health, including workplace wellness programs, corporate social responsibility, and the ethical implications of business practices on health. By examining case studies of successful initiatives, the chapter will highlight best practices and lessons learned.

The chapter will explore the impact of health disparities on economic outcomes. By analyzing the distribution of resources and access to healthcare services, it will highlight the economic costs of health inequities. It will discuss how poor health affects productivity, workforce participation, and economic growth, emphasizing the importance of investing in health to achieve sustainable economic development.

Finally, the chapter will examine the role of health economics in shaping public policy. By exploring cost-benefit analysis, economic evaluations of healthcare interventions, and the allocation of resources, it will provide insights into how economic principles can be applied to improve health outcomes and achieve a more equitable distribution of health resources.

10

Chapter 10: Health Communication and Education

Effective health communication is essential for promoting wellness and ensuring that individuals have the information they need to make informed decisions about their health. This chapter will explore the principles of health communication, including the use of clear and accessible language, culturally appropriate messaging, and the role of media in shaping public perceptions of health.

The chapter will discuss the importance of health education in schools, workplaces, and communities. By examining successful health education programs, it will highlight best practices for promoting health literacy and empowering individuals to take control of their health.

The chapter will also explore the challenges of health communication in the digital age. By analyzing the impact of social media, misinformation, and digital health technologies, it will discuss the opportunities and risks associated with the use of digital tools for health communication.

Finally, the chapter will emphasize the importance of a comprehensive approach to health communication that integrates multiple channels and engages diverse audiences. By highlighting the role of partnerships between health professionals, media organizations, and community groups, it will provide a roadmap for effective health communication strategies.

11

Chapter 11: The Role of Technology in Health

Technology has transformed the landscape of healthcare, offering new opportunities for improving health outcomes and enhancing the delivery of care. This chapter will explore the impact of digital health technologies, including telemedicine, electronic health records, and wearable devices, on patient care and health management.

The chapter will discuss the potential of emerging technologies, such as artificial intelligence, genomics, and precision medicine, to revolutionize healthcare. By examining the benefits and challenges of these innovations, it will provide insights into how technology can be harnessed to address complex health issues and promote wellness.

The chapter will also explore the ethical and privacy considerations associated with the use of health technologies. By analyzing case studies and regulatory frameworks, it will discuss the importance of ensuring that technological advancements are implemented in a way that respects patient rights and promotes equitable access to care.

Finally, the chapter will emphasize the role of collaboration between technology developers, healthcare providers, and policymakers in driving innovation and improving health outcomes. By highlighting successful partnerships, it will provide a vision for the future of technology in health.

12

Chapter 12: Health Systems and Infrastructure

The organization and structure of health systems play a critical role in determining access to care and the quality of health services. This chapter will explore different models of health systems, including public, private, and mixed systems, and their impact on health outcomes.

The chapter will discuss the importance of health infrastructure, such as hospitals, clinics, and community health centers, in providing care to populations. By examining case studies of successful health infrastructure development, it will highlight best practices for building resilient and effective health systems.

The chapter will also explore the challenges of health system financing and resource allocation. By analyzing different approaches to funding healthcare services, it will discuss the importance of sustainable financing mechanisms in ensuring access to care and promoting health equity.

Finally, the chapter will emphasize the role of health system governance and leadership in driving improvements in care delivery. By highlighting the importance of transparent and accountable decision-making, it will provide insights into how effective governance can enhance the performance of health systems.

13

Chapter 13: Global Health and the Social Contract

Health is a global issue, and the social contract of health extends beyond national borders. This chapter will explore the role of global health organizations, international agreements, and cross-border collaborations in promoting health and well-being.

The chapter will discuss the impact of globalization on health, including the spread of infectious diseases, the movement of health professionals, and the transfer of health technologies. By examining these factors, it will highlight the importance of global cooperation in addressing health challenges.

The chapter will also explore the role of global health initiatives in addressing health disparities and promoting health equity. By analyzing case studies of successful global health programs, it will provide insights into best practices for improving health outcomes in low- and middle-income countries.

Finally, the chapter will emphasize the importance of a comprehensive approach to global health that integrates political, economic, and social perspectives. By highlighting the interconnectedness of these dimensions, it will provide a vision for a more equitable and sustainable global health system.

14

Chapter 14: Ethical Considerations in Health

Ethical considerations are central to the social contract of health, and this chapter will explore the ethical principles that guide healthcare practice and policy. By examining key concepts such as autonomy, beneficence, non-maleficence, and justice, it will provide a framework for ethical decision-making in health.

The chapter will discuss the ethical challenges associated with healthcare resource allocation, including the distribution of scarce resources and the prioritization of health interventions. By analyzing case studies and ethical frameworks, it will provide insights into how ethical principles can be applied to address these challenges.

The chapter will also explore the role of ethics in health research, including the protection of research participants, the importance of informed consent, and the ethical considerations associated with emerging technologies. By examining these issues, it will highlight the importance of ethical oversight in promoting responsible research practices.

Finally, the chapter will emphasize the role of ethical leadership in promoting health and well-being. By highlighting the importance of integrity, transparency, and accountability, it will provide a vision for ethical leadership in health.

15

Chapter 15: Health Policy and Advocacy

Health policy plays a critical role in shaping the social contract of health, and this chapter will explore the processes and strategies involved in health policy development and advocacy. By examining case studies of successful health policies, it will highlight best practices for promoting health and well-being.

The chapter will discuss the role of evidence-based policy-making in addressing health challenges. By analyzing the use of data and research in informing policy decisions, it will provide insights into how evidence can be applied to improve health outcomes.

The chapter will also explore the role of advocacy in shaping health policy. By examining the impact of advocacy organizations, grassroots movements, and public campaigns, it will highlight the importance of civic engagement in promoting health.

Finally, the chapter will emphasize the importance of collaboration between policymakers, healthcare providers, and communities in driving health policy development. By highlighting successful partnerships, it will provide a roadmap for effective health policy and advocacy strategies.

16

Chapter 16: The Future of the Social Contract of Health

The social contract of health is constantly evolving, and this chapter will explore the trends and challenges that will shape its future. By examining emerging health issues, technological advancements, and changing societal values, it will provide insights into the future of health and wellness.

The chapter will discuss the potential of innovative approaches, such as personalized medicine, community health initiatives, and health technology, to transform the social contract of health. By analyzing these innovations, it will highlight the opportunities and challenges associated with their implementation.

The chapter will also explore the role of global health initiatives and international cooperation in shaping the future of health. By examining the impact of global health organizations, international agreements, and cross-border collaborations, it will provide a vision for a more equitable and sustainable global health system.

Finally, the chapter will emphasize the importance of a comprehensive approach to health that integrates political, psychological, and business perspectives. By highlighting the interconnectedness of these dimensions, it will provide a roadmap for achieving a more holistic and inclusive social

CHAPTER 16: THE FUTURE OF THE SOCIAL CONTRACT OF HEALTH

contract of health.

17

Chapter 17: Conclusion and Call to Action

The conclusion of the book will summarize the key themes and insights from the previous chapters, emphasizing the importance of the social contract of health in promoting wellness and addressing health disparities.

The chapter will provide a call to action for individuals, communities, and institutions to uphold their responsibilities in the social contract of health. By highlighting the importance of civic engagement, advocacy, and collaboration, it will inspire readers to take an active role in promoting health and well-being.

The chapter will also emphasize the need for ongoing dialogue and reflection on the social contract of health. By encouraging readers to critically examine their own beliefs and values, it will foster a deeper understanding of the complex and interconnected nature of health.

Finally, the chapter will provide a vision for the future of the social contract of health, emphasizing the importance of a holistic and inclusive approach to health and wellness. By highlighting the potential for positive change, it will inspire readers to work towards a healthier and more equitable world.

18

Chapter 18: The Role of Cultural and Social Factors in Health

Cultural and social factors significantly influence health behaviors and outcomes. This chapter will explore how cultural beliefs, values, and practices shape individuals' understanding of health, illness, and treatment. By examining case studies from different cultural contexts, it will highlight the diversity of health practices and the importance of culturally sensitive healthcare.

The chapter will discuss the impact of social relationships and networks on health. By analyzing the role of family, community, and social support systems, it will provide insights into how social connections contribute to well-being and resilience. The chapter will also explore the negative effects of social isolation and the importance of fostering strong social ties.

The chapter will explore the role of social norms and expectations in shaping health behaviors. By examining the influence of societal pressures, gender roles, and cultural stigmas, it will discuss how these factors affect individuals' health choices and access to care. The chapter will emphasize the need for interventions that address social barriers to health.

Finally, the chapter will emphasize the importance of cultural competence in healthcare. By highlighting the need for healthcare providers to understand and respect patients' cultural backgrounds, it will provide a roadmap for delivering culturally appropriate care and improving health outcomes.

Description: "The Social Contract of Health: Political, Psychological, and Business Perspectives on Wellness"

In "The Social Contract of Health: Political, Psychological, and Business Perspectives on Wellness," embark on an insightful journey that explores the multifaceted dimensions of health. This comprehensive volume delves into the intricate interplay between political ideologies, psychological theories, and business practices, highlighting the collective responsibility we share in promoting wellness.

Through 17 thoughtfully crafted chapters, the book examines the historical and philosophical foundations of the social contract theory and its application to health. It sheds light on the role of governments, businesses, and individuals in upholding this implicit agreement to support each other's well-being. From the impact of public policies on health equity to the significance of mental health awareness and the ethical considerations in healthcare, the book offers a holistic perspective on the social determinants of health.

Readers will discover the profound influence of cultural and social factors on health behaviors, the transformative potential of emerging technologies, and the importance of effective health communication and education. With a focus on global health, ethical leadership, and innovative approaches to health promotion, this book provides a roadmap for achieving a more equitable and sustainable health system.

"The Social Contract of Health" is an essential read for policymakers, healthcare professionals, business leaders, and anyone interested in understanding the complex and interconnected nature of health. It calls for a renewed commitment to fostering a healthier world, where political, psychological, and business perspectives converge to create a comprehensive approach to wellness.

www.ingramcontent.com/pod-product-compliance
Lightning Source LLC
LaVergne TN
LVHW020508080526
838202LV00057B/6244